Out
On the Rim
Of the Now

BART MALLIO

Out on the Rim of the Now
Text © Bart Mallio

Cover illustration: © Janine Manheim
Back cover photo © Janine Manheim

Design/Art Direction Lisa Breslow Thompson
LisaThompsonGraphicDesign.com

Library of Congress Control Number: 2022907011
ISBN: 9781941573358

Published by Damianos Publishing
Saxonville Mills
2 Central Street, Studio 152
Framingham, MA 01701
www.DamianosPublishing.com

Produced through Silver Street Media by Bridgeport National Bindery, Agawam, MA USA

First printed 2022

CONTENTS

Dedication

"First of all, every time you begin a good work, you must pray to Him most earnestly to bring it to perfection."
— Prologue to *The Rule of Saint Benedict*, verse 4

This book is for my wife Janine Manheim, and for two friends and teachers who have gone on ahead of me— Celeste Goodridge and Br. William James, OCSO. While I miss having the both of you around, I am a firm believer in the communion of saints.

Room 2, Upper Dorm

09/08/1999 - 07/19/2001

Five Haiku from the Observership

cold afternoon—
one expects chimney smoke
from the beaver dam

the cricket and I
have trouble keeping still
during vigils

screenless windows wide—
a single golden moth accepts
my invitation

rock bridge through
icy rushing winter brook—
the hushed pine forest

dusk by the cornfield—
tree branches rub like birdsong
in twilit wind

(09/08/1999 - 12/09/1999)

My Past

My past
is a network
of spies, hidden behind
The Iron Curtain
from before the War.

No one can tell them
it is over, and,
although I have withheld
their pay, they are patriots,
working only for The Cause.

In dreams, ciphered signals
arrive. Before dawn
I fumble through code-books—
SHE OBSERVED IN LOVE.
MEET ME. WEAR BERET.

They embarrass me—
Lurking near monuments,
trenchcoated, clutching
day-old copies of
Le Monde. And yet,

Loyalties cannot
be ignored— hardships,
past valors, and a dim
fidelity, bridging
the then and now.

(07/30/2000)

Absent Lovers

Perhaps foretold—perhaps
but more likely, accumulation—
a culmination? —of too much
loss, evil, and fear. Broadrick,
bald, clutching a Fender,
would bellow "Pure!"
…I have my doubts.

No longer hip, nor hipster:
older, with suspicions
that rainy nights
and imported cigarettes
are ultimately untenable—
a dry cough
in
the damp dark.

As always, I keep a small room,
neat, and forensically deducible
as belonging to
the formerly caféd.

But, no lipstick traces;
no epic tectonic
shifts.

(12/05/2000 – 05/13/2001)

Abdication from the Planning Department

Thank you, God.
I am too tired
to invent the world today.
I lack the focus,
and there is too much
I would leave out—someone
else's favorite food, someone
else's hit record, the moon
—if I *really* wasn't paying attention,
various birds.
           Today, I am content
to rise at two-thirty, dress,
get coffee, and go to choir…
where there are psalms, there is Darkness.

In the cloister, bugs
buzz and hum,
doing Your will.

(12/07/2000 - 07/14/2001)

The Process of Weeding Out
Novitiate, December 2000

I get out of bed feeling rank,
like something too long in Tupperware
at the back of the fridge.

Alone, cleaning house,
my mind sings
                  songs
in the key   of
            blah blah blah.

Catching myself in a mirror,
I look concerned
at the fact
that I look concerned,

And afternoons become evenings at four.

(12/07/2000 – 05/27/2001)

Crooked Landscape

A stone-fenced road stops
atop one rise, and
behind another.

Beyond barbed wire,
one glimpses a tiny pond,
ducks, and another hill
(higher still than
the one on which you stand
gazing south).

Sweeping up it
is a meadow, bordered
by hemlock,
bald and sharp
against the cold spring sky.

In the trees, a crow croaks,
cows low one field away,
and coyote bones bleach,
glinting,
among the weeds.

(01/23/2001 - 07/01/2001)

An Excerpt from *The Book of Accusations*

...and what about
me? when are the cops gonna
drop outta drop ceilings,
seize me, haul me outta my cell,
kicking and screaming— "this man's a
fraud! Fiend! no monk, no—
only sweaty nightmares and uncouth
cigarettes, a smile like an empty ashtray,
and vomit-proof zippered
combat boots! no! be
not deceived! deep in this moldy
stale-bread heart lurks the thrusting
lust of longing for shapely brunettes,
and espresso! no soul, no—
left gummed to the floor of some dingy
breezeblock ashcan nightclub, still being buffeted
by angry shouts of 'Reagan! Reagan!'
and double kick drum blasts...reading
Swine-born and Bawdy-layer, blowing
smoke at the reflections hanging
in the mirrors of bars, playing, leaving,
and pissing weak vinegar onto roadsides
near blinkered heaps, whose flashers illuminate trunk-fulls
of beer-stained Peaveys and zonked,
inarticulate guitarists.

"Holy, holy, thrice holy!
Beware his darkened vision—
porchlight on the muzzle of a Luger,
a decomposing mathematician
staining a sublet carpet, clutching
his works. Shudder, and breathe his fear—
He alone has survived to tell ye!

"His fingers tremble in the dust of empty rooms,
His fashion is his shroud."

(03/23/2001 - 07/14/2001)

A Poem for Comedians
for John Wieners

For my final performance
I will sit in a chair;
sit in a chair with a hand
in my hair, my pursed,
anxious lips proclaiming, "I care."

For my final performance
I will mop up the floor;
mop up the floor as sweat
drips from my pores, my haggard
brown eyes concealing my core.

For my final performance
I will walk down the hall;
walk down the hall as the
autumn leaves fall, my inter-
laced fingers embracing my all.

Before Vigils, I often
Stop outside to see the stars:
Their light, older than the first
Man, sent to warm
Trilobites in shallow seas.
In my heart
I wish them well, and once,
I waved back.

For my final performance
I will utter one word;
utter one word that's profound
and absurd. The arch of my
eye like a dark ocean bird.

(04/06/01 - 05/13/2001)

Lullaby

Day ends, the last
pallid yellows darken,
flaring on my eastern wall;
my weary clothes are
pegged behind the door.
Stiff sandal-less feet
dangle off the bed, as
silence steeps and pools
in shadows, under tables—
No coughs, no footfalls, just
weak crimson light and
the ticking of my watch
like a sentry beetle.
Dust settles on letters
spiraling down through
little tidal whorls of air.
Sleep claims me, and I
do not resist.

(05/30/2001)

Corpus Christi

It has rained all day, at times in
torrents, great mop-buckets of gray
sluicing-wet drench upended
ceaselessly, tediously, spectacularly
for four hours.
Now, heaving masses of sagging
grey cloud limp the horizon—
The sun a beige blotch in exile
just above treeline—as the night
returns. Birds tick and titter, damp,
flustered, brushy things, eager
for the absent day, but governed
by twilight's inexorable
laws. Monks (in many ways the same)
read in cloisters and cells throughout
Sunday's final hour. Compline
tolls in twenty minutes, and then
psalmody, Salve, Angelus,
a blessing from the Abbot and
bed, beneath thin coverlets in
the humid ick of this hot June.

(06/17/2001)

The Rain and John Cage

I am leery of approximations—
my footnotes, my universal quantum
theories. I hear rain and wind as spare
percussion spattered against a white noise
field, panned left to right in the mix.
But John Cage did not invent the rain.
Backwards it have I—as if Cage wrote "Rain"
and God, hearing it at some ill-attended
college modern music recital,

                              cribbed it,
and snuck it onto the set list under
a pseudonom-de-guerre.

                                However, I do like
this performance: now with the dopplering
jet overhead, now with distinct pitches—
Rain on rain in a rain gutter,
like Balinese metallophones.

(06/20/2001 - 07/14/2001)

Lament

No New Orleans funeral dirges,
No pall-bearing brass band melancholy —
A single piano chord hangs in an upper room,
A branch knocks the window. All the spiders, spinning.
A cough on the ground floor, and then,
The closing of doors.

(06/22/2001 - 07/14/2001)

Boston Subway Vespers

Soon, soon, the grey grit and
acrid smoke of burning
carbons. The raw shimmer
and crush of sidewalks on
blue, cloudless eves. Pleated
wool and nylon swarms blare thru
streets, boiling across
surfaces, heedless, fey.
SRO on the Red
Line, amid whining fans
and the roar of ties in
the maw of a monster.
Dazed and vacant after
fluorescent, flat-screen days,
droned in the flat B-flat
of 60-cycle hum,
now, eyes stir and waken,
evening-blooming, hungry
for beauty's clear respite.
And I, sweaty pin-striped
underarms and belt-looped
technology, smiling,
with the quizzical grin
of O-wot-the-Hell fixed
on my face, I hang on
the burnished rail, waiting,
half-conscious, ears cocked
for the peal of steepled
bells, for the sandal's slap
in the long red cloisters.

(07/19/2001)

Farewell

four boxes, four
bags, bass, amp, kneeler —
leaving Spencer

(07/18/2001)

In Exile,
and
At Home

07/26/2001 – 03/29/2004

In a Season of Drought

I.

Burnished, bright—backhanded
Through shadeless asphalt lots,
Exhausted, leaky-eyed
In the bakey shimmer.

Wasps whine incessantly;
Feet bog and quag in
Prehistoric tarmac.

Nothing is lean, or cool,
Or clear.
                Nothing is still.

II.

Small seacave chambers drenched in
sourceless green-blue-light. The chill:
anticipated autumn.
White wind and noise…
                        The new moon
shelters ice in the hollow
of the rock; the full moon draws
the road among the dimness…

I have got to find the river.

III.

In rivulets, run
and pool in the dust.
Hands upon the spade;
hoarse from shouting off
the crows.
   Just the click
and chuff of the blade,
the raucous croaks.
     Soon,
time and clear water,
treeshade, a whisper
     of
wind.

(08/08/2001 - 07/09/2002)

Morning's Rose Quartz Light

Morning's rose quartz light promises
changelessness, a Sunday stasis
of winter café afternoons,
of late nights in bed alone (with
jazz stealing in like another's
dream from another's room), and in this
dream, frozen rain beats down outside
my window, onto streets and cars…

But it is summer, still, and
this solitary promise will
remain unfulfilled…cities flash
by outside my window, teeming
with commuters and school children;
mist lies low. It will be
                              hot in
D.C., hot and muggy, on these
last two weeks of summer.

(09/07/2001)

Cry

O love me! I am tired
And unable to pray.
I am worn out with tears.

> All my streets are empty;
> Everyone I love has
> Gone home, to bed and
> warmth.

It is late, and the marshes
Are rimed with frost.

(09/10/2001 - 01/08/2002)

Mothlife

Late in the cool of the evening,
mothwings beat the cusp of autumn.
No wind chimes. No moon: leafy blackness.
Moth antennae seek down the lanes,
moth eyes burn reflected lamp-light,
moth breeze wafts from wings like
parchment-pale fans.

Tiny mothfeet alight on wood,
on pebbled wrought iron,
on skin.

And in this interlunar dark,
I glide weightless between streetlights:
Rapt with the seeking.

(09/21/2001 - 11/27/2003)

Departures

Long gone under the summer moon,
Gone with the neap tide, gone, with
Sliver crescent in the dimming
Smoky grey. Gone, with little wavelets
Dwindling into shore, gone, with
Smokestack clouds become sky, and
A prowful of waves become wake.
Gone, and on the damp sand standing,
Waving, smoking. No one. Gone. Gone. Gone.

(09/23/2001)

Greenly, Over the Dam

Greenly, over the dam,
down small falls, beneath stone
bridges (vaulted, lichened,
cool), tumbling under-
ground,
      dripping
into stillness, into
dark spaces:
      sounds unheard.

          What eye surveys this work—
          where it is always late,
          always the town square
          with sharp winds and bright stars,
          where bells echo down the
          empty rails at three a.m.?

(11/19/2001 - 11/18/2003)

For Janine

elegant fingers,
warmth in the marble poverty—
then falling snow

(12/17/2001 - 01/8/2002)

Reading Saint Augustine

At times,
it seems the Holy Spirit draws him aside
like a curtain, and speaks to me directly,
leaning out of his lean frame like a Ghost
in a haunted-picture movie-mansion—
It is frightening: too much intensity
and love, too much knowledge—and then, like a
door slammed shut, he is himself, merely
pious, brilliant, sick with love for the truth,
urgent in his apprehension of grace.

(01/09/2002)

At a Coffee Shop Before Recording, on St. John of the Cross' Feast Day

Pre-studio in the church
of the secular—hot
coffee, old jazz, rain,
morning chatter. Today:
vocals, guitar overdubs.
Chilly wood-paneled lowlight in
the interrogatory
glass control room—Heede
taut above the knobs,
Dilly (arms crossed in
frowning focus),
Noel squinting from
the couch, the blue trails
of cigarette smoke, the whir
of tape across heads, a
slow exhalation. Outside—
the grey rain pools in
mirrors broken by tires,
umbrellas jostle beneath a
leaden canopy, holiday
shoppers,
Sinatra and Crosby welcome
Christmas.
        John of the
Cross, intercede for us.
Bless this our hipster
undertaking. Smile
upon our struggle,
upon the laborious
ascent of scales and
dark afternoon of ceaseless

retakes. In our own small
way, we too welcome
the Child, hoping to make—
if not totality—
at least laughter, hope, the
comradely rush of forward
motion. Christ, grant your
Peace to us who ought
to know better, who
strive as if life
was not gift, who fight
as if the battle
was not yet won. Bless
us with your joy. May we
greet our new creation with
the same enthusiasm
Your Father made us.

(12/14/2002)

For Pablo Neruda

Tonight, I am
the traveler
upon the hidden
errand, whose heels
strike sparks from stone.

My swift passage
unremarked;
my eye true. I
am not shown where
I am bound.
My compass beats
within me.

With my left hand
I pass lightless
through labyrinths.
With my right, seas
break-wave before
me. I am the
messenger and
the message.
Once released,
fleet, I fly true.

Phosphor-bright, I
gaze within
the nether, nitred
chamber, sink knee-
deep into grey
airless moondust,
tread the black basalt
of sunken
Marianas.

I will return.
Stay with me, take
my hand: burn, bold
with this bright
beauty.

(05/15/2003 - 07/23/2018)

Blackout

Two candles, and tea—
Tired eyes drink these
Pale, flickering flames
Seeking clarity.
No lights, radio
TV, internet…
Reading a headache-
Inducing pleasure.
Writing is simpler—
Large blue letters bulge
Between fainter blue
Lines, bold in dim light.

Flashlit motion spots
Half-shapes stretching from
Corners; bright colors
Become a dizzy
Delight. Blind habit
Flips dead switches, and sighs…

Across the street, lights
Traverse blackened rooms
Like revenants, or
Watergate burglars.
The wind—still felling
Trees?—slips through casements
And pokes peevishly
At guttering wicks.

With a pocket set,
I play the Modern
Defense, infin—
itessimally
Trying to take space
From encroaching White.

Would I have written
Tonight without this
Unforeseen stillness?

(10/15/2003)

Dreamwater
(For JMM)

*"75% of Americans are chronically dehydrated.
(This likely applies to half of the world population)"*

At night, must my dream-self
drink great, well-deep dippers,
lest it crumble
into fine
        vermillion
powder,
        and be borne aloft
as eyes for the desert
simoom?
        And how can I
drink it, when the glass keeps
becoming
            a telescope,
and the liquid
                pooling
into a cobalt-and-
                mercury
        moon?

(11/02/2003)

On Being a Bassist

Alone at the
space, all I hear
is fluorescing
sixty-cycle
hum.
       It's late, and
even the true
believers have
packed it in.
               I'm
crashed on white
vinyl, my amp
still buzzing, my
bass still pressing
down on my chest.

On a piano
bench become
coffee table—
my metronome.
I drink lukewarm
water (a rest).

Twenty years, now—
countless evenings
wreathed in smoke,
stolid in dark
repose beside
the drummer. My
hands thrum the tune's
pulse, push its blood,
fill its lungs, dance,

and exhale still
caesurae.

My great reward:
to know so much
of time, of the
space inside
movement, of sub-
divided breaths—
bright, exploded
instants outside the
compass of clocks
and watches…to
gaze upon
the curve of sound
from isolate
distances, out
on the rim of
the now.

(11/24/2003 – 11/30/2003)

Golden Woman

golden woman, I am
drawn by your scents— pale
vanilla breath, metallic
tang of sweats…drunk
on your mouth, I kneel
before the perfect arching
of your neck.
           my fingers'
whisper-trace against your
skin is faint music, past
midnight, when only wind
and moon remain.
             time slows
to a glacial age
of caress and sigh.

(01/07/2004)

Song for My Bean

Before the rosy-fingered dawn,
I rise and wash and put clothes on.
I walk beside the quiet stream,
I go to tell my bean my dreams.

My bean is special, my bean is true—
My bean is radiant in hue.
The sun uncurls her lustrous leaves;
Her meadow hums with drowsy bees.

At noon, I lay aside my pen;
I wander to the river's bend—
I sit beneath her purple shade,
I sing small songs within her glade.

My bean is mine, and I am hers.
I touch her green and supple curves.
She strokes my cheek with softest leaf—
I fear no pain, I own no grief.

Past dusk, I light a lantern pale,
And sit upon the streambank's shale.
I open books of ancient tales,
And read aloud 'til lamp-light fails.

At night, I curl around my bean.
We fall asleep beside her stream.
The starlight falls through cloudless skies
To kiss her lovely lidded eyes.

(01/20/2004)

At Twilight

At twilight, all
The crabs march up
From the wine-dark,
Purple surf, bearing
Pebbles and green
Seaglass. Before
Moonrise, tiny
Tidal cathedrals
Break the surface
Of the landlocked
Pools.
        Putting your
Ear to the sand
You can hear them
Softly singing.

(01/21/2004)

Fragment I

Half-past winter, dead February's ice,
Blue, burnished aluminum skies blankly,
Baldly proclaim a season of austere
Solitude.

(02/08/2004)

Mass Ave. and Brookline, Cambridge, MA

Pink clouds diffuse sun into sourceless light—
no sharp shadows, just blurry blackness below
feet as they fall on crosswalks. Cellphones abound.
Outside Hi-Fi Pizza, dudes in hoodies
laugh and smoke, warding off Monday morning.
Kids in mo's proclaim "Ramones!" with stenciled
leather. Two wanna-be MCs trade rhymes
outside Central Convenience (the nappy one
has skillz). Hey Mark, it's changed some since
that thunderstroke smote your heart mid-song in Rome.
You can't smoke in bars. Heavy metal came
back. Cambridge gave you a square, a little
one. There's a nightclub on the corner, and
the booths are full of kids drinking cheap beers,
digging their peers, and dreaming up band names
throughout these cloudy Sunday afternoons.

(03/02/2004)

O Antiphons

Ordo Fratrum Minorum keeps these
Orange flames lit—some electric,
Others touched alive by hand.

Oxygen and prayer forge smoke
Out of orisons, bearing our
Oblations upward, beyond
Opacities, anxieties…

Oasis, Origin, honor
Oaths struck with your people—bread, wine,
Oil and water re-form us—
Ordain us—as bringers of your peace.

(03/09/2004)

East,
by
Water

06/30/2004 – 12/12/2006

Summer Rain

It is enough,
sometimes— hearing
summer rain, late,
in blue darkness,
shirt off, barefoot.

(07/19/2004)

Wedding Song

Fading light on wind-driven blue
waves. Gulls hover and wander
outside above the empty bay,
as my new wife lies sleeping.

Mid-autumn beneath a setting
sun, a gold more burnished than leaves,
redder than copper, embrazened,
as my new wife lies sleeping.

Slowly, sundial shadow
inscribes the room within the arc
of its stately, tranquil compass,
as my new wife lies sleeping.

The earth turning as the gulls turn,
the moon rising as the tides return
to this still, dusk-hushed center—
where my new wife lies sleeping.

(11/06/2004)

For Robert Creeley and Philip Lamantia

Through occultation, we learn
by eclipse. Lesser bodies
interpose themselves
between us and a source
of light (often one too bright
to be observed directly). We
then augur via penumbra
and aura, intuiting the thing
by its inextinguishable
traces…
        Insomniac, caffeine-addled,
web-surfing, I learn belatedly
of your deaths, rapt in the blanket
of spring's black chill.
                 Three rooms away,
my ticking clock continues.
                 I reach first
For Love, and then, *Ekstasis*.
Dressing, I find my green notebook,
and put up the water for green
tea.
    I will wake you
           first, with your
poems, and later,
       with my own.
            For me,

the paradox is
        incarnational—
the presence of the obscure, the
inexpressible, the transcendent
in the revealed,
        the articulated,
                the words.

(04/11/2005)

Pilgrimage

Muffled in mist, I see
the running lights of neighbors'
houses, tree trunks like
buoys, and a white door
bobbing in the backyard.
                              (No
bells, alas, or fog horns.)
My refrigerator
thrums instead, and coffee
percolates, and lends its
song to water dripping
from the eaves.
                    I am cold,
on this watch, but unwilling
to wake my wife while rummaging
for a sweatshirt.
                    Today,
we are bound east,
where dew-haze mixes with
salt-fog in an airborne
estuary.

        No sound
will mark our passage, and
the landscape will be writ
in silverpoint and ink wash.
At the island's margin
we will take our bearings,
and then continue on.
                    All
good things arise in
secret, from silence.

(12/26/2005)

Cleaning Up the Town

I would stand alone,
at the far end of a
single dirt street, and
                 hitch back
my serape.
                 Drawing out
the empty, long barreled
revolver, I would point west,
and ask, "Are these not unlike
the mountains Basho saw,
crossing into Shirakawa
three centuries ago?"

(12/28/2005)

Test Pattern

All things have unity— in simile,
at least— with associations providing
a timeless narrative of translation
and approximation— orange becomes
baseball becomes pinstripes becomes business—
until P. T. Barnum stands, in wingtips,
and a black cravat, talking pitching with
Yogi Berra, who, pushing back his mask,
bites down on a thick rind of Floridian
fruit, so his thick fingers can gain purchase,
and yank the husk off the thing, which comes away
whole, like the cover of a foul ball unlaced
by Shoeless Joe Jackson, sometime during
that final triumphant season, before
the ignominy and defeat. Kahlo,
perhaps, could grant this moment unity—
the sunlike orange, the grey pinstripes, the
meaty fingers, the black stovepipe hat.

(01/26/2006 – 07/04/2009)

The Call
of
the Shakuhachi

02/03/2006 – 10/28/2019

The Call of the Shakuhachi
for Beth Lowell

The stillness of the day…
so few sounds indicate
motion. Most are electric—
radiators, lights,
refrigerators. Only
the tea kettle links me
to a natural world.

                                    I
have gone inside, somewhere,
down a narrow, fern-edged
path, paved with loose stones, to
a small hut, by a pond
full of koi. Sitting in shade,
I hear a bamboo flute
from across the pond. In
my mind, I cannot gauge
if there is a flautist
or if that is just the sound
of that place, woven in
to the uncoiling fern
leaf, the round yellow mouth
of the koi, the shadow cast
by the roof-edge, the flat
strikeplane of the path's rock.
Inside, there is coolness,
a faint smell of pine, the
damp of thick plank after
a night of rain. And,
a single note, stepping
across the pond and onto
the hut's small porch, to visit.

Outside, there is snowless
winter…a sort-of night-long
conversation between
spring and fall, who, like friends
who know better, have
elected to stay up
past their bedtimes, and
visit, trading old stories
and poking (desultorily)
at a peevish fire.
Perhaps they, too, are
on a porch by a lake.
They know they will be
tired in the morning,
that they will go to work
reluctantly, and yawn
all day, covering their
gaping mouths with backed
hands, shaking their heads,
and smiling ruefully.
But they are confreres,
and besides, winter was
detained, and the least they
could do was to keep watch
thru the night. Maybe,
they would hear a pickup
turning onto the gravel road
off the paved interstate,
and see halogen light
break across the trunks of
pine trees. A door slam, and
then big boots sinking into
the needle carpet, as

someone approached the house…

But not now. Outside, a
lonely purple flag flaps
unenthusiastically.
A forgotten hammock hangs
in a corner of the
yard, bearing a precious
cargo of brown and yellow
leaves. A white door peels
genteelly, propped-up
against an oak trunk
below the purple flag. From here,
one story up, in the kitchen,
seen through gauze curtains,
I am reminded of Pooh
and Christopher Robin,
of Moomintroll and
Snuffkin, of Frog and Toad.
Who lives inside that door,
within that tree, flying
that flag, resting in that
hammock? Are they asleep,
dreaming of spring, of green
buds and grass, of gentle
rain on flowerbeds, of
returning birdsong, and
violets? Did they forget
to take in their flag, or
is it a reminder
of springtime, a little
banner of hope, so that
their friends, who, stirring and
yawning and galumphing

to the edges of burrows,
could look out and be cheered,
before turning over
and going back to sleep,
not unlike a Christmas
tree glimpsed through a train
window by a haggard
commuter, late on a
cold December evening,
clutching the *Times* and a
worn leather satchel with a
buckled brown strap? He must
render unto Caesar before
this final quarter ends,
but he knows that Christmas
will come first, a week early,
and that somewhere in their
apartment, his wife waits,
under a blue blanket,
dark hair pillowed on an
armrest, while a man
in a stiff white chef's coat makes
a perfect mousse on their
television. The train
hoots at crossings, not unlike
an owl, hooting on a
branch beside the purple
flag, or an owl startled
by headlights on a gravel
road to a lakeside cabin,
or like a note from a
bamboo flute drifting across
a twilit summer pond,
or like a tea kettle

murmuring to itself
on a second-floor stovetop
in a Long Island home.
Two rooms away, my wife
sleeps. She is sick, and her breath
whistles a little in
her nose (like a little
flute, or a stainless-steel
tea kettle atop an
electric range). She sounds
like a small brown bird
cheeping on the northeast
windowsill of our study.
I miss her, miss her cold
hands and nose, the long limbs,
the lovely smile
on the golden skin…but,
she must rest, hibernating
this snowless winter day
away, like my neighbor
in his tree-trunk home, with
its white wooden door and
purple flag, flapping slowly,
in the little gusts of
wind that rattle the leaves
in the hammock, or blow
sparks from the lakeside fire,
or bring the call of the
shakuhachi across
the surface of the
mosquito-dappled pond.
The wind blows where it
pleases. We hear its sound,
but we cannot say where

it comes from, or where
it is going. A traveler
on a snowy rail-line
returning to his wife
hears it rattle casements.
I see it now in the small
shapes it makes in a
forgotten purple banner.
It is like rain on the
surface of a pond, when
the fish rise up to feed
and their large orange mouths
move very slowly, open
and shut, like bellows, and
the listener hoists his
hams and calves up, swinging
them south, so they are
on the porch, under the
awning. The birds fall silent,
ferns bend under the drops,
and the call of the flute
ceases, somewhere across
the pond. At the lakeside
cabin, the fire sputters,
and the clearing is filled
with the scent of pine needles,
and music like little bells
as the bed of the cooling
pickup dings and dongs when
nickel-sized drops of water
clong onto it. The friends
laugh, and move inside. Behind
the white door, my neighbor
dreams of drops spattered across

April's lilacs, and the
business traveler
thinks ruefully of
his Jetta, at Huntington
Station, surrounded now
by melting snow and slush.
I love the rain. It is
a song played for everyone,
bridging cities and counties
and states, such that Paul, at a
casement in the Old
Executive Office
Building in Washington,
answering his cellphone
as he gazes southeast
towards a mist-shrouded
White House, can cough out a
monosyllabic laugh, and
drawl, "Yeah. It's coming down
pretty hard here, too," while
deep in New Jersey, east
of Williams' beloved
Patterson, Beth (sitting
still in a screened porch
amid the sudden onslaught
of rain) can say quiet,
soothing things to an antsy
Border Collie. I find
the rain is better
than radio.
                    Inside,
it makes sense that the flute
stops only for the rain.
But for the traveler

it is an obstacle,
a fresh challenge— at best
a variable, at worst
treachery, a snare for
the unwary, and a
barrier to peace. Rain
wars against you until
you arrive, and then it
cradles you in solitude,
drawing its curtain of
mist about your windows
like a cloak.
                    Three seasons,
on a porch at a cabin
on a lake in my mind,
all bond with rain. It is
fall's harbinger for winter,
and winter's harbinger
for spring. My neighbor
behind his wooden door
would fall asleep in cold rain,
and wake in warm rain. Really,
if his hibernation
is sound, his dream of winter
may be a dream of rain,
a dream of cold water
imperceptibly warming
three months' time, with snow
being an effectless
cause, a phenomenon
whose manifestation
can never be observed
but must be theorized about
during spring's youngest days...

Furry theologians
with bright, black, beady eyes
argue snow's divinity,
with zealots on either
side, chucking acorns at
each other's heads. A wise
bear (who woke lean and hungry
one January,
and wandered out into
a twilit Sunday snowfall)
keeps her own counsel. She knows
she cannot say if the
snow caused itself to fall
or if it was sent by
another, only that
it was very, very
beautiful, and that, sometimes,
the recognition of mystery
is beauty enough.
                            Meanwhile,
in this apartment, I
stretch languorously in
my kitchen chair, and listen
to other water sounds—
the thrum and rumble of
water in a kettle,
and the burbling pop
of water in the
humidifier, two rooms
away. Both change water
into steam, curling up
in ectoplasmic wisps
to banish the desert
brought on by baseboard heat

and February cold.
One gives me tea, the other
helps my wife to sleep.

                      Soon,

she must wake, and a new
chapter will begin— I
will cap my pen, and close
this notebook.

                  The rain upon
the fern-edged pond will stop,
and I will have to take
the narrow path from the hut
to the exterior.
(I wonder, who feeds the koi
when I am away?)

                    The sun
will rise over the lake;
spring and fall will depart,
and leave the cabin, the pines,
and the pickup to winter.

My neighbor will awake,
and his dream-season of
contemplation will be
replaced by mundanities
(mostly involving food).

The weary winter traveler
will return, remove his
dripping galoshes, and
warmly embrace his wife

even as I will warmly
embrace mine, give her tea,

and ask how she is
feeling. There will be trips
to mailboxes and to
Mass, videos from
the town library, and
egg drop soup.
                              Elsewhere,
a lean bear will settle
in a cliffside cavern
covering her coal black nose
with her broad black paw,
and doze, and dream
about snow, and the wind
(which blows where it pleases)
leaving only echoes
in its swift passage
under the winter moon.

(02/03/2006 -10/20/2019)

The
Traveler

09/03/2007 – 04/02/2012

Middle Age
(for Sharon Gaddoniex, on her 40th birthday)

Are now all our revels ended?

Some say youth lies in the choosing,
and our choices are mostly made.

Some say youth lies in rebellion,
but we have reached a troubled peace.

Our days are heavy with blood and bread,
flesh and loam. We have become our dreams,
and they have surprised us
in their comings-true.
                Now, the hard work—
the long, tricky passages through
the icefloes, alone in the wheelhouse
in the dead of winter's night, the crew
turning in their bunks below.

We are become the watchmen, and
around us, a city slumbers
full of others' dreams, young and old,
entrusted to us. We light our lamps,
and walk the battlements among them.

No longer afraid, we gird ourselves.
Unpaved, the road stretches into
the distance, towards empty peaks
each of us will climb alone.

(09/03/2007 – 09/13/2007)

The Day Columbus Discovered America
for Lawrence Ferlinghetti

The day Columbus discovered America
I was on the Long Island Railroad to Brooklyn.

The day Columbus discovered America
it was overcast, and the streetlamps burned pale blue.

The day Columbus discovered America
I had a sandwich, an orange, and an apple.

The day Columbus discovered America
the Yankees were losing to the Indians.

The day Columbus discovered America
I woke at 4 a.m. to feed a hungry cat.

The day Columbus discovered America
I reassured a Russian about privacy.

The day Columbus discovered America
I dozed as an Englishman manipulated sound.

The day Columbus discovered America
I ate frosted kosher sweet rolls and drank green tea.

The day Columbus discovered America
the morning subways were empty of students.

The day Columbus discovered America
I read a haiku about a horse eating roses.

The day Columbus discovered America
a wolf spider watched me with eight bright eyes.

(10/08/2007)

Glimpsed from a Train
for Austin Grossman

Glyphic picture-names,
rusting rooftop grills
(forgotten since when?),
weed-choked gravel
at generator
stations, wind-haunted
backlots, track-access
trails disappearing
in sassafras and
gorse.
     Sidings:
half-completed
tasks and downed tools (like
coffee mugs steaming
in the galley mess
of the *Marie Celeste*).
Glimpsed, in pockets—
a future where we
have left,
       and left behind
signposts, pointing up
and down the line
of continuity,
between what was
and what is to come.

Not all these places
exist (not yet), or
can be reached by
walking the tracks back,
in heavy boots, town
by town.

Tell me, spirit, are
these shadows of what
is,
   or of what
is to come?

(10/18/2007)

For Janine

We lean against each other at the play,
Too old to counterfeit a Montague—
For Monday's ruins Wednesday may renew,
And dark clouds scatter 'ere the close of day.
Nor could we countenance a Capulet,
Concealing truth behind a masque of death—
Unmoved while weeping parents placed a wreath
Upon our vain and selfish monument.
Our reason whispers sweetly to our passions;
Our friendship buoys injuries and slights.
Holding ourselves aloof from fads and fashions,
Long days apart converge in gentle nights.

(04/08/2008 – 01/23/2019)

Exhortations for Artists
for Chuang Tzu and Henry David Thoreau

Seek the shape of ancient mountain birch!

With unrestrained gaze,
                                reach out of thin earth
into the fulminating Heavens!

With one half, dance unfettered in the storm!
With the other, drink the mountain's root!

Bend unbreaking branches beneath
March's mix of snow and frozen rain.
Blossom in bunches of ivory florets—
Clusters of milky lace and filigree—
whose chartreuse leaves
                                imperceptibly
deepen to mossy malachites.

As moon illuminates the lichens,
welcome the Emperor, the Sphinx, and
the Lime-Hawk upon your branches.

Blaze gold and burn a verdigrised bronze,
each leaf unique and freely given.

Know contingency—
                                your coming-forth
unmistakably singular, and
molded by hands
                                Other than your own.

With knots and knobs, deflect the axe—
Persistence grained in every twist and vein.

Above all, be useless—
Fit companion to hawks,
avens, boulders, foxes,
switchgrass, tarns, and the
ruminative bear.

Burst forth in glimpses!

(08/19/2009 – 8/29/2009)

Fragment II

lowering clouds erase
an equality of light

the unlaid rails reflect
neither glint nor spark

(09/22/2009)

Tempus Fugit

I have nothing to say
and am saying it...so,
I should be done

                    already.

(01/08/2010)

The Cloud

Stillness engrained
in my resting
body.
        A dark
peace
            ringing clearly
in my resting
mind,
        like a bell
forged of smoke
from the incense
brazier.

All smoke rises;
all bells ring.

(01/12/2010 – 01/23/2019)

Vector
for Bill Dixon

Words trickle
Each sound a shimmering drop
A moment of
           intention
A pivot point--
         alone,
              distinct,
In space.
        A sound, or
             sounds
Swinging free
        in the air
Until
    --context--
          a meaning.

Then, shooting off
           into
              the interlunar dark,
       on course.

A single trumpet note--
bent as it fades--
in a dark practice room
in a college conservatory
late, late at night.

(01/19/2010)

Pastiche for John Ashbery

Our tourism cut short by weather, we
returned at once to the Babel Hotel.
The head waiter graciously seated us
in a garden of hibiscus and beets,
the sated vegetation redolent
with a francophone longing. Our graven
images smile secretly, fingers
covering their mouths, like giggling geishas
or movie actors with bad teeth. It seems
we can do nothing right during these short
windy afternoons of cloud-studded
concupiscence. Everyone is always blaming
his neighbor for the unpaid water bill.
You know this, and have seen it on the bus—
the furtive eyes darting like trapped spring moths,
the fingers curled tightly around '60s
baseball card collections. Everyone wants
particulars— makes, models, license plates,
years, colors, even the shape of the dent
in the front quarter panel. It exhausts
me—the mail-in quizzes, the Tupperware,
even the lawn wants to know, "How'm I
doin'?" Yet all this too has the feeling
of something pre-paid and long-forgotten
arriving through the post, a dim message
from the past, like last year's tie on back-order,
a credit card charge we vigorously
dispute, but must ultimately accept.
The court stenographer reads back the minutes,
and the records are sealed. We knew it would
come to this, to sweaty armpits and not
quite getting what we want, like birthday gifts

from maiden aunts. Now the train is leaving
and we must get on board—cry "Adieu!" to
the big city and wave bravely to those
standing on the platform, our hands caged
like little birds.

(01/29/2010)

Wilderness of Mirrors

O wilderness of mirrors
A breadless waste of self
No brackish streams flow east
Toward some greater river.

Only a mirage of others —
A veiled threat, stony laughter,
Peripheral phantoms,
The wind among the rocks.

This graven image — blasted,
Baked, forgotten, until
The self we worship is
Obscured from all memory.

What will the wind say?

Something knocks upon our doors
Bone on wood, demanding
Payment, and we pretend
That we are not at home.

If only water or bread,
Or wine, or a traveler,
Bound with us along this road —
Night is coming on soon...

What will the wind say?

(02/05/2010)

For Brother William James, OCSO

Dawn finds me
pen in hand at the close
of vigil.
          My praise
is to write new psalms.

I long to be
the cathedral in which
His Word is chanted.

The words fall
and coat the morning ground
like manna
              or dew,
soundlessly with us.

I long
to search for them each dawn—
always just enough.

(02/09/2010)

Instructions

Go now, to where the map and magnetic
poles merge, by the secret way; mark yourself
with ashes and bring nothing. There is a crossroads,
and a man with keys and a lantern. He
awaits you, with a map only you can
decipher. Go now, thru midnight streets of
silent shops and sleeping burghers. Go now,
as the patrol warms itself and smokes.
Go now, past the outpost, and through the zone
of rusted wire and neglected tank-traps.
Go now, past the frontier, and the desert
beyond, to the inner mountain. The moon
is new, the stars are bright, the compass true.
Go— the one you love awaits only you.

(02/20/2010)

Lenten Poem for Evagrius
for Brother Paul Henry, AA

I am a lens, a lesser copy
of the One who focused me
into being. What I take in
becomes part of me, changes me—
into what?
                    I do not choose well.
I choose things that place me
in the center, my small concerns
radiating out, illuminating
a small, dirty room I call home.

I do not choose well.
                    I argue
with myself, defeating my foes.
I triumph over imagined
adversity. I am revealed
to others as consequential.
I leap from burning wreckage. I
champion justice for others.
I tip the scales.
                    I...
                    I...
                    I...
I am a creature. I cannot
invent more of me. I cannot
staunch the flow of time. I cannot
raise the dead, or give them a home
in Eternity. I need help
making the subway on time. I
could lose some weight. I get winded
running up flights of stairs,

and this
will usurp Creation? Will lead
armies into battle? Refute
skeptics? Break open stony hearts?

I do not choose well.
I fill when
I should empty. I withhold
when I should give. I take umbrage,
forgetting my own unkindness.
I speak when I should listen, judge
when I am wanting, celebrate myself,
and sin myself...

Forgive me: I do not choose well.

(02/22/2010)

HER

I flee from HER across the ruined castles of dawn
Scrambling through abandoned banquet halls and over
      broken masonry HER searchlight eyes setting
          rotting
      tapestries ablaze,
My skin bubbles like burning pitch, my eyes
      of agate sting with the scent of lilacs
I am sought by HER murder of burning crows
      whose light outshines the moon and whose
      dark flame eclipses the sun, their
      ravening beaks open
And their shriek fills my ears with the cries
      of a thousand snot-nosed idiot children
      bellowing only for the love of HER
I am a purple bruise, a sprained muscle,
      a broken lamp, a heelless boot
But HER beauty swims before my eyes
      with the radiance of ignited hydrogen
And I am whirled into dust to be born aloft
      on the wind of HER wings.

(03/25/2010)

The Errand

O King
we have been lost
these many years

The broad road has
become the faintest track
and we cannot return

We have failed you
on our errand, and we wander

And our clothes are rags
and our banners tattered
and our boots without heels

We cannot rest
or stand still— your work
burns within us like a coal
and will not let us be

So many strange customs
and tongues, so many
unfamiliar stars

O King
we hope this missive
reaches your court one day
we are so sorry

Please find us
and take us home

(07/27/2011)

Listening to Billie Holiday and Lester Young
(for Eric Arrington)

It arrives like a black and white postcard
of a white orchid wreathed in grey smoke.

First, canary silk quickens your skin
and deceives it, so that the fine-grained
sandpaper of truth abrades your soft pores,
raising redness and leaving little
pinpricks of blood raw on the surface.

And with this blood, you make pact
with every dingy furnished walkup
that served a grave for hope.

From the bridge's rail,
you step forward out over the river
                              but you rise,
slipping free from every judge and cabaret card.

The rain in pools reflects the stars.

(08/15/2011)

For My Mother on Her 80th Birthday

The debts that we incur accrue in ways
we do not observe directly, like shells
which always seem to be upon the beach.
The wavelet strands them reluctantly,
and then withdraws. They are beyond its reach
like a toy the kitten seeks beneath
the couch. They always seem to have been there—
glittering on the sand, rough or polished,
free for the taking. So casually found,
they seem less than a gift; so plentiful,
we take them as granted. And one fine dawn,
bluebright, brisk, shrill with wheeling gulls above
the broken prism of the waves, they shine—
we know distinctly each spiral and curve
haloed for once in singularity.
The tightening coil of sacrifice,
intention, and love as visible as
the church's spire, glimpsed from a clearing
on a wooded hillside, leading one home.

(10/11/2011)

Early Gotham Mornings

02/23/2010 – 05/04/2010

Sonnet for Thomas Merton

Who knew your seven-storey mountain would
lead me to my vocation— married life?
That in the cloister I would glimpse my wife
as patiently she pigmented the wood,
and Christ emerged to bless us with His peace?
In hindsight, acts of seeming random chance
reveal themselves as steps within a dance,
but one that does not let the dancer cease
from dancing...that commitment is a choice
we must re-make each day, like sailboats bound
for distant ports, their mainsheets tightly wound,
their lookouts keen and ready to give voice
as soon as land is sighted. You steered true.
My heart is willing, God's ocean vast and blue.

(02/26/2010 – 02/28/2010)

Longjing Cha

Outside,
        rain rings
thin, distinct tones
from windowpane
marimbas and
drainpipe bells—
        bright
tin jades and dark
glass malachites—
spatterings in
spare, unmeasured
time...
        Inside, warmth
shimmers from vents;
heat ghosts ripple
red tablecloth,
captivating cats...

Appliances
thrum long, low drones
a nickel's-width
of pitch apart...

The winter kitchen
steams with spring—
long, yellow-green
leaves give out a
pale amber brew,
filling the room
like rising mist
off a rain-soaked
mountainside
in eastern China.

Bare cool feet flat
on bare floorboards,
notebook open,
pen uncapped,
I take my first
sip—
　　heat flushes
my face, there is
a slight sweetness
at the center
of my tongue, and
an astringency
at the back of
my throat.
　　　My nose
opens, and I smell
plum blossoms amid
the melting snow,
and hear the wind
shake the willows
across the water
on the dark shores
of the long lake.

(03/03/10 – 03/05/10)

Passed Lives

Crowded into a booth in a small bar,
a host of faces whom I have not seen
except in decades' worth of dreams. The green
and yellow light leaks in, with sounds of cars
and passersby upon the noontime street.
It seems they have nothing to say to me—
our time together past, they are now free
to flicker, and dissolve like winter sleet
becoming water. I am grateful, still,
for time with them, and miss them keenly now—
their farewell eyes fixed upon the black prow
of their strangely graven ferry. A chill
pervades, like dust motes in an empty room.
A lonely juke box plays— slow, and out of tune.

(Spring of 2010)

Cyberdefense

An early Thursday, coffee hot and black,
I sit beneath fluorescent lights and watch
reconnaissance attempts, a blundered hack
from rural France...when, flaring like a match,
some compromised computers wake, and try
to blast our websites off the 'net. They fail,
predictably. But, timed to coincide
with this attack, a single piece of mail
arrives— a program masquerading as
a picture. Open it, and your PC
will relay all your data to Hamas.
I forward this to spies outside D.C.,
assemble logs, then type up my report,
and hope we face this hacker in a court.

(Spring of 2010)

Road Song
(for Saint Francis of Assisi)

Don't stop to count the cost of what is fair,
Be generous with what you cannot keep—
You'll never have enough, so why not share?

Grain fills its shape with soil, sun, and air—
Not everything you sow is what you reap.
Don't stop to count the cost of what is fair.

Sometimes cold barley broth, and half a pear;
Sometimes grilled sausage made from pigs or sheep—
You'll never have enough, so why not share?

You may go hungry, bent double with care,
You may tread lightly, on heights or through the deeps—
Don't stop to count the cost of what is fair.

You may beg your fellows for subway fare,
Or stretch your legs in limousines and sleep—
You'll never have enough, so why not share?

In moonless dark, or summer's noontide glare,
On roads gentle, or treacherously steep—
Don't stop to count the cost of what is fair.
You'll never have enough, so why not share?

(Spring of 2010)

What I Learned from Television
(for Allen Ginsberg)

I don't know...
is America worth
it? All I can tell is
someone is selling me
a car.
     Everyone wants
wealth, and sexual health,
and a God who is just
like them.
       They want to be
immortal, and to live
without fear, in modest
ease.
     What they really want
is to see themselves
on television:

       Race
should only matter when
it is transcended by
the socially aware.

Women are beautiful,
but they should stay in their
places
    (except when they
must Heroically Save
the Day).
     Men are artless
lunkheads,
       overweight, dim,

but well-meaning
                    (except
when they have a Dark Past,
or must Save the Day,
                    or
are gay...)
              Women, too, can
be gay, when they are
                        beautiful
and men can see them kiss
their girlfriends.
                But, gay men
must be single.
                Old people
exist to possess wealth,
or care for grandchildren,
or be homeless prophets.
They cannot have sex,
                    unless
they were hippies,
                and are
wealthy and defy
                convention.

Children are good for smart-
aleck remarks, and strange
undiagnosable
diseases, and being
kidnapped
            (hence the term).
As teens, they will struggle
with social acceptance
in new schools, with love and

sex, with substance abuse,
and with gang membership.
Lucky teens will either
fight ancient vampires,
or date them.

Serial killers roam
the land, preying on you
and me, apprehended
by Technology in
the hands of sardonic
cops-turned-scientists.
                              (Most
Technology is bad,
except when it catches
serial killers.)
                    (Most
cops are sardonic,
intolerant, macho
nitwits,
              except when they
have personal crises, or
use forensic science
to catch serial killers.)

All corporations are
bad.
      They exist to burn
the rainforests, and hide
toxic waste in our kids'
playgrounds.

They meddle with
Technology
           (which turns
into robots who
                      enslave
humanity
           (except
when it is used to catch
serial killers)).

           Life
and death happens in
hospitals, where doctors
and nurses frantically
fall in and out of love.
This
      —and the unfair loss
of nice people's lives—
is their burden.

           Now, the
Government is tough to
explain.
           They are evil,
conspiratorial
warfighters, serving the
wealthy, brokering deals
with aliens,
                 except
when there are terrorists,
or serial killers,
or when the President

is a Democrat.
                 God
exists to be doubted,
or turned away from, as
when one becomes a
scientist, making new
Technology, which will
enslave us, but may catch
a few serial killers
along the way.
                 You can't
believe in God and still
do science, as the only
purpose of science is
to accidentally
enslave humanity.

All social ills are found
in the lives of immigrants
and the very, very
wealthy.
                 Lawyers, in two
thousand-dollar suits from
the District Attorney,
will explain them to us.

Married women tend to
struggle with their lunkhead
husbands, and dominate
other married women.
Their relief from all this
comes from smoldering

                    affairs
and from their best friends who
are often strangely single
gay men.
            (A
word of caution, ladies—
sometimes, these secret boy
friends are serial killers
who will take you hostage
and must be caught with
                    Technology.)

If you are murdered, though,
never fear—sardonic
intolerant, macho
cops will bring your serial
killer to justice.

(Spring of 2010)

Downshifting

04/03/2012 – 05/11/2020

After Moonrise

I have been lying
on the oak floor
of the abandoned house
since midnight.
                        After moonrise
there were voices
on the stairs,
                footsteps
and a door that kept
slamming.
                I am waiting
to hear the song
the piano makes
when its strings vibrate
in sympathy
with the wind through
the mushroom's gills
and the neap tide—
when Aldebaran
stands above
the horizon.

(04/03/2012)

Facing East in Hicksville

Facing east in Hicksville,
it occurs to me that I
have grown lazy, drifting
on a Sargasso current
of minor triumphs,
trivia, and tribulation.

I don't care about money,
and the country doesn't care
about itself. I love Christ,
and my wife, and beauty.

The vague, unraveling,
clamorous counterclaims
of moral impurity
shrilly squeaking at me
from social media
just can't hold my interest.

People should mind how they treat
each other now, while we're
breathing. We'll all be dead
soon enough, and our crimes
will come to light, anyway.

I need to strike out—
away from the radios
with their fresh disasters,
into those small, furnished
rooms of the heart, with their
peeling-paint windows, their
Cross on the wall, their lumpy
futon into which
I may tumble with my
beautiful wife.
      An easel
for her, a desk for me,
and a cat to keep
the windowsill warm.

(07/01/2012 – 10/21/2019)

Lantern

for Sharon Paice, on her 50th birthday

I have lost count
of the hours spent past midnight
on the steps of summer porches,

of the lukewarm mugs of herbal tea
balanced on amps in rehearsal studios,

of the ecumenical salons
and the kinship of dreams,

of antiquarian bookshop hoards,
and deep-fried Vietnamese spring rolls,

of the ecstatic prayers
catapulted toward Heaven
on the wings of a sound system,

of small kindnesses
and companionable silences.

Your heart is a lantern lit
in a farmhouse window
cheering the weary traveler
leading his fogdamp horse
long after sunset
across the rolling, empty moorland.

(07/30/2010 – 07/31/2012)

Holiday

The damp sand
weighs the cuffs
of my pinstripes

Filtered silver light

Wind-rippled
chaise lounges

Towels half-buried
on the strand

Soundless gulls

Skeletal umbrellae

The empty curve
of the bay
into sunset

Where night will never fall

The bungalows wash
up and down
                        up and down
into the placid
violet sea

(07/13/2012)

The Back Garden at Sunrise

Whistler dawnscape—
Violet and cerulean
impatiens emerge,
as pools of shadow shrink,
evaporating
imperceptibly
like sidewalk puddles
after summer thunder.

Terre verte surfaces—
lost emeralds glinting
in a firepit. Leaves
motionless, bared
by an ebbtide of
darkness. Umbers warm.
Iron is burnished,
faint luster sparkling
its pitted surface.

Cinabrese flowers
resolve into shapes,
no longer ghosts of
candleflame wavering
in a milori world.

Waxy ivy cups
light, making tiny
false flowers from
highlights at the center
of its leaves. Insect
wings become translucent.

The underside
of a falling leaf
hints at taupe—
today's first bit of
ochre.

(07/23/2012 – 05/11/2020)

The Gregorian Custos
for Steve Callahan

Silence begins sound,
which blooms lily-like—
milk erupting
into black coffee.

After the churning,
slowing, suspension—
equilibrium:

The long tones you hear
sitting past sunset
in a darkened room,

Like dust settling
in tiny bookstores
in closet-sized
offices, painted
battleship grey, lit
fluorescently,
tiled black and
yellow,

Like the whirr and click
of changing traffic lights
heard in passing
long after midnight
at summer's empty
intersections.

(01/04/2013 – 01/06/2013)

Paddle to the Sea

Some of my life
is like a boat
set free on a stream
by a boy
who does not know
that it can never
return to him.

(09/12/2016)

Hourglass

I never learned
the names of trees, or colors,
or the songs of birds.
Is there still time left to speak
Intimately about life?

(07/31/2017)

Laziness

To get more coffee, or
to just sit, listening
to the whirr of
the impeller of
the humidifier
pushing water into
the atmosphere?

(03/06/2018)

Statement of Work

Poetry is the parking lot
of an office building in an
unfashionable neighborhood
of Orlando, Florida, where,
standing at the driver's side door
of your rental car in summer
twilight, you may gaze unfocused
at the building's adobe roof,
suddenly alive with the
darting emerald green
of tiny chameleons.

(03/06/2018)

Laundromat
(for Saint John Henry Cardinal Newman)

There are days
I am afraid
That I lost my soul
By accident
In a laundromat
In Cambridge, Massachusetts.

That I'd left it
In a pair of jeans
And it tumbled out
And wound up
Forgotten
At the back
Of a dryer.

Do you think
It might still be there,
Somewhere, behind
A paper packet
Detergent dispenser,
Stuck to old gum
And lint?

I hope it's not lonely
On long quiet nights
When the neon sign
Buzzes and hums,
And everyone else
Has gone home.

At the time,
I was busy
Trying to be something,
And I didn't
Take good care
Of my things.

Sometimes,
Walking winter streets,
I wonder
What I should have done
With the time I spent
Laughing too loud
At my own jokes.

(12/02/2019 - 04/23/2020)

NOTES ON THE POEMS

This is the first of two volumes of poetry written between 1999 and early 2020. It is primarily focused on poems written in Western poetic forms including open forms. To my mind, these poems easily arrange themselves into seven little sections, each rooted in a particular living space, landscape, and period of my life.

Room Two, Upper Dorm

These poems were begun while I was an observer, a postulant, and a novice at Saint Joseph's Abbey in Spencer, Massachusetts, living amidst members of the Order of Cistercians of the Strict Observance. What I learned at Spencer—the Liturgy of the Hours, *lectio divina*, contemplative prayer, a devotion to the Rosary, and so much else—is still a vital, daily part of my life. In addition, I began writing poetry for the first time in 15 years.

I would caution the reader that my poems from this period are by no means reflective or "typical" of the monastic experience of actual Cistercian monks—rather, they reflect an individual coming to terms with himself while being exposed to and shaped by years of Catholic monastic tradition. Evagrius Ponticus, in his work *The Praktikos*, provides some insights into what is really going on here.

"Absent Lovers" – The "Broadrick" here is composer, guitarist, and singer Justin Broadrick.

"A Poem for Comedians" – Vigils is the first office of the Catholic monastic day; at Saint Joseph's Abbey, it was celebrated at 3:30 a. m.

In Exile, and At Home
These poems were begun as I built a new life on the foundations given to me by my monastic experience. I had sold almost all my possessions prior to entering Saint Joseph's, and I found myself with no furniture, a handful of books, and my electric bass. I began working again as a management consultant and a computer security practitioner. I continued to write poetry and briefly returned to playing electric bass.

"Mass Ave. and Brookline, Cambridge, MA" and "O Antiphons" were written under the tutelage of Moira Linehan and originally published in the chapbook edited by Rosemary Sullivan: *Reading, Writing & Rhetoric: Collected Works from the Year of the Poet, 2003 – 2004* (Winchester, MA: Winchester Public Library), 2004.

"Mass Ave. and Brookline, Cambridge, MA" – a "mo" is an old punk shortening of the word mohawk, as in a mohawk haircut. The City of Cambridge had recently designated this intersection "Mark Sandman Square." Mark was the voice and bass behind the band Morphine.

"O Antiphons" – the Franciscan friars are the Ordo Fratrum Minorum.

East, By Water
I moved to Long Island, where I worked as an information technology manager and information security practitioner. Shortly thereafter, Janine and I were married at Santa Susanna in Rome.

"Lament," "On Being a Bassist," "The Rain and John Cage," "For Robert Creeley and Philip Lamantia," and

"Dreamwater" were first presented in 2007 as part of a video reading for the website poetryvlog.com, curated by Michael Mart and George Wallace.

"Test Pattern" was on display as part of the Connections show in the gallery at the East Ends Arts Council, Riverhead, New York, in June of 2013.

The Call of the Shakuhachi
My good friend and fellow poet Beth Lowell was challenged by a poetry instructor to write a 500-line associative poem which would dare to encompass everything she was experiencing at the time. Beth passed this challenge along to me; here is my 354-line response.

The Traveler
These poems were written as I commuted to and from Manhattan as an information security practitioner. Many of the poems from this period were written either as occasional poems, or "in dialogue" with other artists and their work.

"Exhortations for Artists"—avens are tiny flowers native to the Cascades and the Rocky Mountains. A tarn is a small mountain lake left in a glacial cirque. The emperor, sphinx, and lime-hawk are all species of moths.

"Lenten Poem for Evagrius"—Evagrius Ponticus (345 – 399 AD) was a Christian monk and theologian, and author of several early works on monastic spirituality, including *The Praktikos*.

Early Gotham Mornings
Between late February and early May 2010, I participated

in an on-line poetry class taught by Michael Montlack at the Gotham Writers Workshop. The focus was on formal challenges, and the resulting work seemed unique enough that I felt it deserved its own small section herein.

Downshifting

These poems are from a later period where I found myself accompanying people I loved through hardships and losses, which required the power and traction that comes from shifting into a lower gear.

"The Gregorian Custos" — In Gregorian chant, a custos is a note that appears at the end of a line; it is not meant to be sung, but it alerts the singer to what the first sung note will be on the line that follows.

ACKNOWLEDGMENTS

Thanks to both my family and my wife's family, for all their love and support. Special mention must be made here of my Aunt Mary and Uncle Michael, and my Aunt Osee, who nurtured my love of reading and writing with an unstinting generosity. And, thanks are due to the monastic community of Saint Joseph's Abbey, in Spencer, Massachusetts, where this book has its genesis.

Thanks must also be extended to a handful of very close friends who have encouraged this work in its many stages— Doug Church, Whispering Deer, Sharon Gadonniex, Br. Paul Henry, AA, Fr. Isaac Keeley, OCSO, Sharon Paice MacLeod, Fr. James Palmigiano, OCSO, Paul Shawcross, and Br. Adam Zielonka, OCSO. And, for those folks who help keep body and soul functioning together— Jim Fanara, Tom Lorio, Jim Mahfuz, and George Masone.

This book would not be possible without the community of writers I have learned from, especially Maryann Calendrille, Judy Hession, Michael King, Greg Lenczycki, Moira Linehan, Beth Lowell, Michael Montlack, Stevan-Adele Morley, Andrea Pawley, Gerry Skinder, Rosemary Sullivan, Kathryn Szoka, and Noel Ventresco. Nor would it be possible without all the individuals with whom I have been lucky enough to play and study music—for me, these two art forms are deeply intertwined.

ABOUT THE AUTHOR

Bart Mallio was first introduced to poetry by his parents.
An elementary school lesson in haiku taught by local poet
Stevan-Adele Morley introduced him to a form he would
revisit throughout his life. He later attended Bowdoin
College, where he majored in English Literature and
History. In addition to poetry, he has performed
extensively as an electric bassist. He lives on Long Island.

PER GRAZIE RICEVUTE